For many centuries, Christians around the world have celebrated the birthday of Jesus through music, drama and song. As children participate in this happy tradition, they extend the joyful spirit of Christmas.

Christmas Is a Happy Time

by Jane Belk Moncure
illustrated by Frances Hook

Distributed by Standard Publishing,
Cincinnati, Ohio 45231.

THE CHILD'S WORLD

ELGIN, ILLINOIS 60120

Distributed by Standard Publishing, 8121 Hamilton Avenue, Cincinnati, Ohio 45231.

Library of Congress Cataloging in Publication Data

Moncure, Jane Belk.
  Christmas is a happy time!

  SUMMARY: Sketches the background and celebration
of Christmas.
  1. Jesus Christ—Nativity—Juvenile literature.
2. Christmas—Juvenile literature.   [1. Christmas]
I. Hook, Frances.   II. Title.
BT315.2.M62   232.9'21   80-17258
ISBN 0-89565-171-8

Christmas Is a Happy Time

"And thou shalt have joy and gladness;
and many shall rejoice at his birth."
—*Luke 1:14*

Christmas is the birthday of Jesus.
Choir bells ring a merry song.
Jesus was born on Christmas day,
born in Bethlehem, far away.
Happy birthday, baby Jesus!

Light the candles.
Let them glow,
as we remember long ago
when God's own Son was born.
Happy birthday, baby Jesus!

Play the story,
the Christmas story,
as we remember
the little Lord Jesus
with Mary and Joseph
in the stable.

11

Come, as angels came long ago
to tell of Jesus' birth —
singing songs of joy and gladness,
"Glory to God; peace on earth."

Come quickly,
as shepherds came
from the fields
to worship Jesus,
the babe in the manger.

Come, as Wise Men came from afar,
following the special Christmas star,
bringing gifts of love for Jesus.

Come, bring your birthday gifts
to honor the time so long ago
when God's own Son was born.

19

Come, let's make gifts for others,
for Christmas is a caring time . . .

a time when we show kindness,
because we remember the birthday
of Jesus.

Christmas is a happy time,
a joyful, birthday-party time,
when carolers sing,
"Joy to the world; the Lord is come."

Christmas is a giving time.
We give surprises to each other.

Christmas is a loving time.

We show our love for one another.

Thank You, God, for baby Jesus,
for Mary and Joseph in the stable,
for the angels, the shepherds,
and the lambs,
for the Wise Men and the star.
Thank You, God, for Jesus' birthday.
Thank You, God, for Christmas.

About the Artist

Frances Hook was educated at the Pennsylvania Museum School of Art in Philadelphia, Pennsylvania. She and her husband, Richard Hook, worked together as a free-lance art team for many years, until his death. Within the past 15 years, Mrs. Hook has moved more and more into the field of book illustrating.

Mrs. Hook has a unique ability for capturing the moods and emotions of children. She has this to say about her work. "Over the years, I have centered my attention on children. I've done many portraits of children. I use children in the neighborhood for my models. I never use professional models."

A great admirer of Mary Cassatt, an American Impressionist, Mrs. Hook enjoys doing fine art as well as commercial work.

About the Author

Jane Belk Moncure, author of many books and stories for young children, is a graduate of Virginia Commonwealth University and Columbia University. She has taught nursery, kindergarten and primary children in Europe and America.

Mrs. Moncure has taught early childhood education while serving on the faculties of Virginia Commonwealth University and the University of Richmond. She was the first president of the Virginia Association for Early Childhood Education and has been recognized widely for her services to young children.

She is married to Dr. James A. Moncure, Vice President of Elon College, and lives in Burlington, North Carolina.

Mrs. Moncure is the daughter of a minister and has been deeply involved in Christian work all her life.